St Davids Ca...
A welcome from...

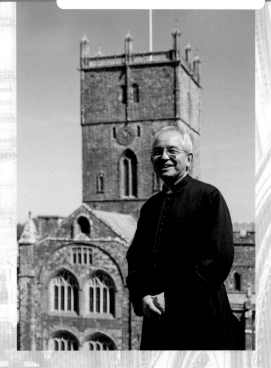

It can be easy for a modern tourist to forget that this extraordinary place is not merely a series of historic buildings in a beautiful landscape. St Davids Cathedral is, above all, a living church and a centre of faith that has attracted millions of people for almost 1,500 years. Everything you see here is a visible expression of the worship of God. Over the centuries, it has been a retreat from the outside world, a centre of power and wealth, and the scene of turmoil and decay. Today, the cathedral lies at the heart of a vibrant community encompassing the city that bears its name, the nation whose patron saint lived and died here. Visitors and pilgrims have found peace and a new sense of purpose in this place of prayer and contemplation. Thousands of people visit St Davids Cathedral and enjoy the beauty of the building and its surroundings, but I want them to do more than that. It is my hope that the recent restoration of St David's Shrine will help to transform the ministry we are able to offer here and 'turn our visitors into pilgrims'.

May God give you his blessing as you leave this place.

The Very Reverend Jonathan Lean

Opposite: The magnificent exterior of St Davids Cathedral.

THE NAVE

The nave, the oldest part of the cathedral, dates back to 1181, when work to replace David's original monastery began. Bishop Peter de Leia and Giraldus de Barri ('Gerald of Wales'), Archdeacon of Brecon and a canon of St Davids, were excused from the Third Crusade in order to complete the cathedral.

The conjunction of round and pointed arches reminds us that the cathedral is a Transitional Romanesque building, its master masons moving only slowly away from the Norman towards the new Gothic style. The many departures from the vertical and horizontal indicate not only the difficulty of the ground beneath – an old river bed –

Above: Local schools gather in the nave to celebrate Ascension Day with Bishop Wyn.

Above: This beautiful rood hangs in the nave; it was designed in 1931 by W.D. Caroe.

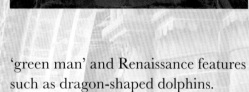

Right: The view along the nave to the west door.

but that the builders probably had to work round the buildings of the old monastery which were still in use.

The magnificent 16th-century roof, created in oak rather than stone, was a response to these structural irregularities. Its decoration features medieval motifs such as the 'green man' and Renaissance features such as dragon-shaped dolphins.

The nave aisles were much lower than they are today. To let in more light, Henry de Gower (Bishop 1328–47) raised the side walls to accommodate larger windows. The blocked space below the wheel window in the south-west corner is a legacy of the previous situation.

It was Gower, too, who built the magnificent stone screen separating the nave from the quire. His tomb lies within it. The figures on the screen are modern, and include a statue of St David dressed as a Norman bishop.

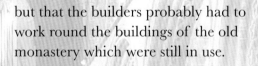

Left: In this modern statue St David is portrayed with a dove. During his address to the synod at Llanddewi Brefi in the 6th century, a white dove is said to have settled on his shoulder.

THE QUIRE

Beyond the screen is the quire, the heart of worship in the cathedral. Here the *cathedra* or throne of the Bishop of St Davids stands, probably constructed by Bishop Gower in the 14th century. Almost 9 metres (29 feet) high, it was once decorated with angels and saints, which can still be seen above the central seat.

The choir stalls were constructed in the late 15th and early 16th centuries. The cathedral is run by a body of clerics known as the Dean and Chapter and here, beneath the tower, each member of the Chapter has a stall.

The names on the stalls are those of the prebends: churches or manors which once provided an income for the clergy whose stalls they are.

Clergy seating at St Davids is different from that in other cathedrals: the Dean sits on the north side, where the Precentor would normally sit; the Bishop has a stall in the quire where the Dean should be; and for unknown reasons, there is a stall for the reigning sovereign. HM Queen Elizabeth II has sat here four times: in 1955, 1982, in 1995 – when she gave city status back to St Davids – and again in November 2001.

Right: An organ has dominated the quire since the 14th century.

Right: A trumpeting angel on the organ parapet.

Left: A concert featuring the Boys' Choir and Lay Clerks of the cathedral.

Several features reward closer inspection: the carvings on the bench ends, the original coats of arms which survive in six stalls, the small carved faces amid the tracery behind the stalls, and the stalls themselves with their misericords – medieval tip-up seats designed to support clerics who were obliged to stand for long periods.

Above: This misericord depicts seasickness, demonstrating the wit of the 16th-century craftsmen.
Opposite: The tower lantern ceiling.

High above the quire soars the tower. Its western supporting arch is rounded, while the other three were rebuilt in the pointed Gothic style after the tower collapsed in 1220. Bishop Gower added a further stage (the lantern) while the upper stage dates from the 16th century.

For centuries the western arch, unsound after an earthquake in 1247, had to bear the weight of these additions. In 1648 Cromwell's dragoons made things worse. With puritanical zeal, they smashed the stained-glass windows, stripped the lead from the roof, ripped brasses from tombs, burned books and removed at least one of the bells, damaging the tower to do so.

Right: The current organ was the first to serve both the quire and the nave.

By 1860 the tower was in a parlous condition, and Sir George Gilbert Scott was called in. He rebuilt it all, giving it foundations where none had existed before and inserting tie-rods to hold it together. Since 1865, it has been largely sound, which has stabilised the rest of the building. Nevertheless, in 1931 it was judged unwise to place a new ring of bells in the tower; instead they were set in the

original 13th-century detached bell tower adjacent to Porth-y-Twr – the only surviving gatehouse in the wall that once surrounded the city.

The organ is the first among several down the ages to serve both the quire and the nave. It was constructed by Henry 'Father' Willis in 1883 and rebuilt in 1920–21, with hydraulic engines replacing manual blowers, and again in 1953. The organ was rebuilt once more in 2000 by Harrison and Harrison, with a case designed by Peter Bird of Caroe and Partners.

A BEAUTIFUL REVIVAL

Legend has it that Dewi Sant (St David) was born locally, the son of St Non and Sant, a prince of Ceredigion. The cathedral stands on the site of the principal monastery of the many communities he founded. He and his monks spent their time in prayer, study and hard manual labour. David rose to become an abbot and bishop, later the patron saint of Wales. He died in 589 and the monastery is said to have been 'filled with angels as Christ received his soul'.

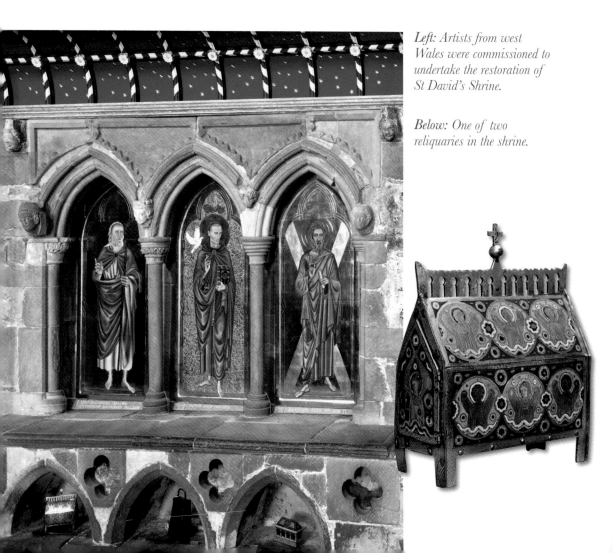

Left: Artists from west Wales were commissioned to undertake the restoration of St David's Shrine.

Below: One of two reliquaries in the shrine.

Left: The icon of St David.

flocked: to obtain divine help; to give thanks; to fulfil vows; or to do penance for wrongdoing. All this ended precipitately with the destruction of the shrine in 1538 at the Dissolution of the Monasteries.

In 2010 an appeal to restore the shrine was launched and on 1st March 2012, St David's Day, the idea became a beautiful reality. The five icons of saints with local connections – David, Andrew, Patrick, Non and Justinian – were created by local artist Sara Crisp.

The canopy, made by Friend Wood to designs by Peter Bird, seeks to replicate a 13th-century construction, and the carvings along its outer edge relate to different aspects of the saints depicted in the icons beneath.

The niches, once for kneeling pilgrims, house two reliquaries, reputed to contain the remains of St David and St Justinian, and also a replica of a 'bangu' bell, used by Celtic missionaries to call people to prayer.

During the 12th century, Pope Calixtus II declared St Davids a place of pilgrimage and David's shrine became a place where hundreds of thousands of pilgrims

THE PRESBYTERY

Even a cursory look at the presbytery reveals a complex architectural history. Some supporting piers are round, some octagonal, while none of them match the arcades; the walls have been heightened; the floor tiles by the altar are 16th century, while those near the shrine were made for Sir George Gilbert Scott's 1863–1901 restoration. The magnificent wooden roof dates from the 15th century.

Sir George did his best to preserve archeologically important features. He rebuilt the four lancets above the altar,

Above: The high altar in the presbytery.

taking out the large 16th-century window which had replaced them. As the large lancets behind the high altar were necessarily blocked following the construction of Holy Trinity Chapel, he installed fine mosaics, designed by Hardman's and executed by Salviati.

Resolutely in the centre of things stands the tomb of Edmund Tudor, Earl of Richmond (died 1456) whose body was moved, at the Dissolution, from its original burial place in Carmarthen. The father of King Henry VII and the half-brother of King Henry VI, Tudor gave his name to a royal dynasty. The tomb stands awkwardly in terms of services at the high altar. Its brass is a copy of that stripped off by Cromwell's men. Thanks to their actions, by the mid-17th century the presbytery and, indeed, most of the cathedral, was in a parlous state. The arches here were blocked up, the aisles beyond being open to the sky.

THE HOLY TRINITY CHAPEL

East of the presbytery, and directly behind the high altar, lies the Chapel of the Holy Trinity (that is, God the Father, God the Son and God the Holy Spirit).

Just as Bishop Gower had built the screen partly to house his own tomb, so Edward Vaughan (Bishop 1509–22) constructed the chantry chapel in which he would eventually be buried. It had an inauspicious beginning, being originally an open courtyard filled with rubbish. The work cost the Bishop fourpence, a large sum of money at the time.

His chapel, built in the Perpendicular style, is lined with oolitic limestone and features superb fan vaulting. Restored in 1923, it is used regularly during the week for early morning services and the Eucharist, as indeed are all the other chapels

in the cathedral. The unusual altar was created by W.D. Caroe from fragments of early Christian monuments, medieval stonework and the original altar slab.

The window openings by the altar allowed the chantry priest celebrating mass there to follow the progress of masses being conducted in the Lady Chapel and the Chapels of St Nicholas and St Edward the Confessor, so that all could keep in time with one another.

Opposite: The altar of Holy Trinity Chapel was reconstructed from medieval fragments.

Right: The fan vaulted ceiling

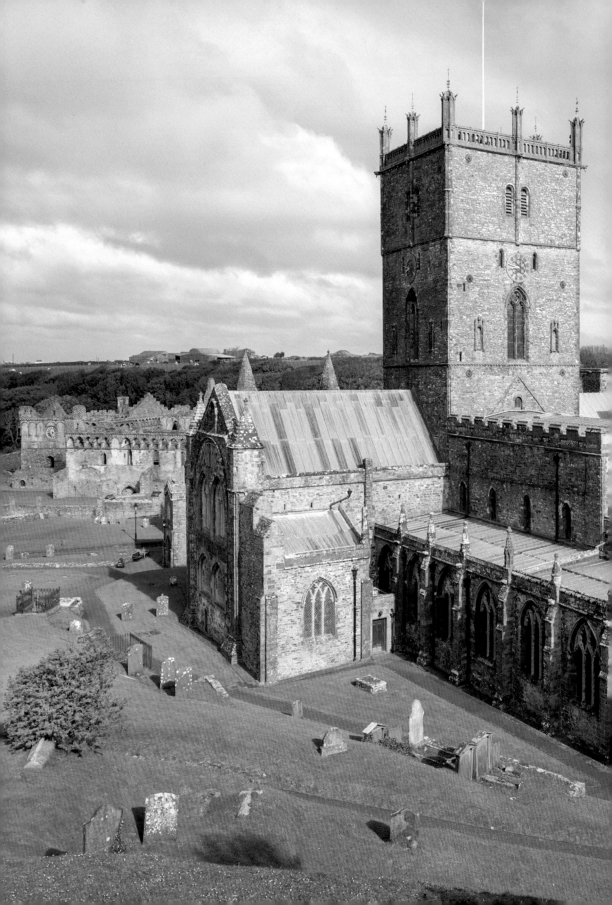

Once Cromwell's men had removed the lead from several roofs on those fateful few days of 1648, it was inevitable that the areas beneath would fall into ruin. The south chapel aisle suffered this fate, and had to wait until 1907 to be restored and re-roofed. The work was paid for by the Countess of Maidstone (died 1932), granddaughter of a former Bishop. She is buried in an elaborate, if slightly incongruous, tomb in the Chapel of St Edward the Confessor in the far south-eastern corner of the cathedral.

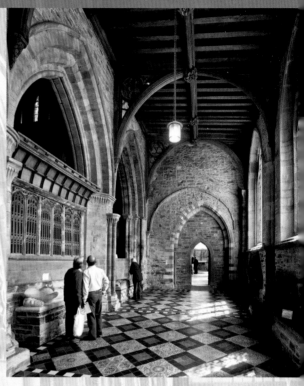

Above: Sunlight creates patterns on the tiles in the south aisle.

On the south side of the presbytery are two effigies of earlier Bishops: Anselm le Gras and Iorwerth, who in 1215 became the first Welsh Bishop of St Davids for over a century. Iorwerth was the author of the oldest surviving set of statutes for the cathedral. In previous times, it was common for a cathedral's

Left: The icon of Elijah being fed by ravens, one of the scenes from the prophet's life.

diocesan and parish roles to be kept separate geographically, and in 1844 the architect William Butterfield was instructed to convert the south transept into a parish church for the community. Scott's restoration did away with this and in the 1950s vestries were constructed in the space. For today's visitor, the transept is distinguished mainly by a beautiful 17th-century icon from Crete

Above: The Chapel of St Edward the Confessor.

Above: One of the tombs in the presbytery.

depicting the Old Testament prophet Elijah being fed by ravens.

It is unsurprising that no building earlier than the 12th century survives at St Davids. All that remains from the pre-Norman period is now included in the exhibition in Porth-y-Twr.

THE LADY CHAPEL

L ady chapels – spaces devoted to the Blessed Virgin Mary – appeared in many important churches in the 12th and 13th centuries. Traditionally these were the largest of chapels, usually placed at the east end and centrally.

In its long history the Lady Chapel at St Davids has seen a great many alterations and additions. Completed in the early 14th century with five or six bays, it may originally have been a detached building, perhaps a 'well chapel' – the holy well lies just beyond the east wall.

Right: This carving of the Virgin and Child is from Germany and is in 14th-century style.

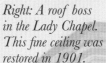

Right: A roof boss in the Lady Chapel. This fine ceiling was restored in 1901.

Bishop Gower added the sedilia and the tombs later in the 14th century and, nearly 200 years later, Bishop Vaughan remodelled it into a Perpendicular two-bay building with a vaulted ceiling – only for Cromwell's men to rob the roof of its lead in 1648. The inevitable collapse came in 1775 and for two centuries the chapel lay roofless. In 1901 it was restored by Gilbert Scott's son, Oldrid.

Several surviving roof bosses are 16th century, while the stained-glass east window (1924) is by Kempe, the Tudor-style stalls (1950) were designed by A.D. Caroe and the alloy and glass entrance screen (1979) was created by Frank Roper.

The cathedral's Welsh congregation meets in the Lady Chapel for Sunday worship.

Left: The Lady Chapel.

With only threadbare resources, the cathedral's 18th-century canons rescued the transepts from their roofless state, but further work was essential in many places. Amongst his other alterations, architect William Butterfield in 1844 inserted the large Perpendicular-style window in the north transept.

Under the tower arch is the tomb of Caradog, a 12th-century saint. It is thought his relics are still in the tomb.

Situated in a bay of the transept is St Andrew's Chapel, restored in the 1950s as the Pembrokeshire War Memorial Chapel; a page in the Book of Remembrance is turned over every day.

In the north-east corner of the transept is the Chapel of St Thomas Becket, built in the 13th century and remodelled by Gower in the 14th. Maybe as part of his penance, Henry II came to St Davids to attend Mass in 1171, the year after Becket's murder. The chapel's ceiling bosses are of very high quality. On the south wall is a fine Early English piscina, a basin for post-Mass ablutions.

Left: Chapel of St Nicholas, located in the east end of the cathedral.

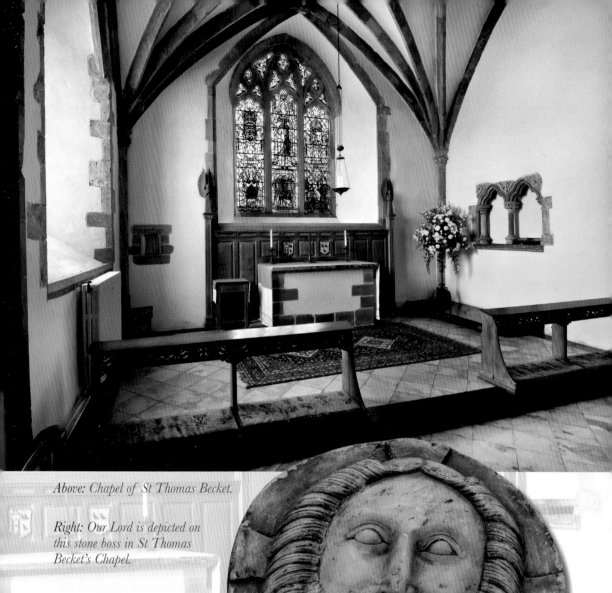

Above: Chapel of St Thomas Becket.

Right: Our Lord is depicted on this stone boss in St Thomas Becket's Chapel.

Above the chapel was the medieval chapter house, where the canons met regularly to conduct the business of the cathedral. This became the cathedral library in the 1950s. Above it was the old treasury where the cathedral's liturgical plate and books were kept. In the 18th and 19th centuries these two storeys housed the cathedral's grammar school.

Today the Treasury, now an important visitor feature (see page 24), is located on the west side of the north transept.

The Treasury

Magnificently displayed, the cathedral's treasures tell the continuing story of 1,500 years of Christian worship at St Davids. Amongst them are important discoveries from the graves of early bishops: beautiful gold rings, silver chalices and, most importantly, gilded copper croziers – staffs of office echoing the pattern of shepherds' crooks which were carried by bishops of St Davids 800 years ago.

Also on display are wonderfully embroidered altar frontals, stone figureheads and a bishop's cope (ceremonial cloak) worn at the coronation of Queen Victoria in 1838.

Right: This crozier is one of the remarkable relics in the Treasury.

Above: A visitor enjoying the displays in the Treasury.

The Cloisters

S ite of a 'college' of clerics founded in 1365 and dissolved in 1549, the cloisters were left to crumble. By 1700 they lay in ruins and remained so for centuries. But now, in the 21st century, they stand magnificently transformed.

St Mary's Hall now houses The Refectory, a restaurant with a stunning mezzanine level; and the Cloisters Gallery, a showcase for high-quality arts and crafts. Beneath are rehearsal rooms and other valuable cathedral facilities.

Above: The cathedral viewed from the cloisters.

The cloisters themselves have been re-imagined in oak and stone – a delightful marriage of old and new which echoes the medieval yet provides the cathedral with a superb 21st-century asset.

Above: The Refectory is a delightful place in which to take refreshment.

Above: Visitors of all ages enjoy The Refectory in its peaceful setting.

AROUND THE CATHEDRAL

Above: The cathedral from the south-west.

Like so much of the cathedral, by the 18th century the west front needed reconstruction. Earlier repairs to the nave had not solved the problems of a sloping and waterlogged site – the front had not only moved almost a metre (3 feet) from perpendicular but it was still going. Around 1780, the architect John Nash (who later famously created much of London's West End) was called in to rebuild it. However, the work, in Gothic Revival style, did not resolve the structural problem.

Above: What better time to visit St Davids than when the daffodil, the national flower of Wales, is in bloom.

Right: The south-east view of the cathedral from Porth-y-Twr.

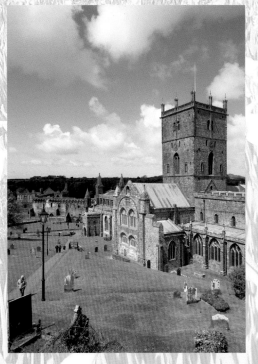

It was only Scott's masterly rebuilding of the tower which stopped the rot. He then turned his attention to the rest of the cathedral, culminating in the replacement of the west front as a memorial to Connop Thirlwall (Bishop 1840–74) who had largely instigated the restoration work. This is what we see today.

Nearby are the ruins of the Bishop's Palace, probably the finest domestic building in Western Britain. Here many royal pilgrims and other distinguished visitors lodged.

A 14th-century wall with 5-metre (16-foot) battlements once surrounded the medieval city of St Davids. Only one of its four gates survives: Porth-y-Twr, 'the tower gate'.

Above: Porth-y-Twr.

Left: The Abraham stone, one of the displays in Porth-y-Twr.

The octagonal portion of this was built to house the cathedral bells when the central tower of the cathedral was two stages lower than it is now. Since 1931 the bells have once more rung from here, and further bells, added for the Millennium, now peal out with a Royal ring of ten bells. Porth-y-Twr now houses an exhibition introducing visitors to the history and life of the cathedral today.